COOL

OPTICAL ILLUSIONS

CREATIVE ACTIVITIES THAT MAKE MATH & SCIENCE FUN FOR KIDS!

ANDERS HANSON AND ELISSA MANN

A Division of ABDO
ABDO
Publishing Company

VISIT US AT WWW.ABDOPUBLISHING.COM

Published by ABDO Publishing Company, a division of ABDO, P.O. Box 398166, Minneapolis, Minnesota 55439. Copyright ® 2014 by Abdo Consulting Group, Inc. International copyrights reserved in all countries. No part of this book may be reproduced in any form without written permission from the publisher. Checkerboard Library™ is a trademark and logo of ABDO Publishing Company.

Printed in the United States of America, North Mankato, Minnesota
062013
012014

PRINTED ON RECYCLED PAPER

Design and Production: Anders Hanson, Mighty Media, Inc.
Series Editor: Liz Salzmann
Photo Credits: Anders Hanson, Shutterstock

LIBRARY OF CONGRESS CATALOGING-IN-PUBLICATION DATA

Hanson, Anders.
 Cool optical illusions : creative activities that make math & science fun for kids! / Anders Hanson and Elissa Mann.
    p. cm. -- (Cool art with math & science)
 Audience: 008-012.
 Includes bibliographical references and index.
 ISBN 978-1-61783-822-4
1. Optical illusions--Juvenile literature. 2. Visual perception--Juvenile literature. I. Mann, Elissa, 1990- II. Title.
 QP495.H26 2014
 152.14'8--dc23
                     2013001896

CONTENTS

COOL

OPTICAL ILLUSIONS

TRICKY IMAGES

Optical **illusions** are images that play tricks. They fool your eyes and brain. When your eyes see an illustration, they send information to the brain. Your brain puts the information together. It realizes that what your eyes saw can't be right!

There are many types of **illusions**. Some look like real objects, like the picture above. Look closer! It could never truly exist.

Some illusions seem to move. Stare at one of the stars below. Watch the other stars rotate.

SEE IT! BELIEVE IT?
TYPES OF OPTICAL ILLUSIONS

PHYSIOLOGICAL

A **physiological illusion** occurs when your eyes are **overstimulated**. Your eyes make up shapes and colors that don't exist.

HERMANN GRID

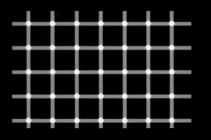

Can you see black dots inside the white circles? They aren't really there!

AFTERIMAGES

Stare closely at this image for 10 to 20 seconds. Then look at a white surface. What do you see?

AMBIGUOUS

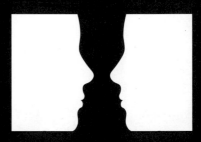

Is this an image of a vase? Or is it two faces?

COGNITIVE

Cognitive illusions begin in the brain. Certain arrangements of shapes can trick the brain. The brain assumes things about the image that aren't true.

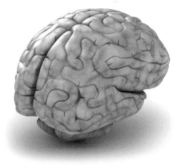

PARADOX

This shape looks like it could exist as a real object. Take a closer look!

DISTORTING

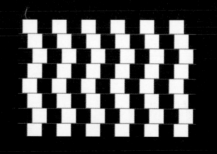

None of the lines in this image are **slanted**. Hard to believe? Check it with a ruler!

FICTION

Is there a white, curved triangle on top of the other shapes? Or is it your imagination?

COLORS
FREQUENCIES OF LIGHT

Colors are organized by frequency of light. The brain assigns colors to certain frequencies. Low-frequency light looks red. High-frequency light looks violet. In nature, a rainbow shows the range of light frequencies. Colors and their frequencies can even be plotted on a line.

VISIBLE LIGHT

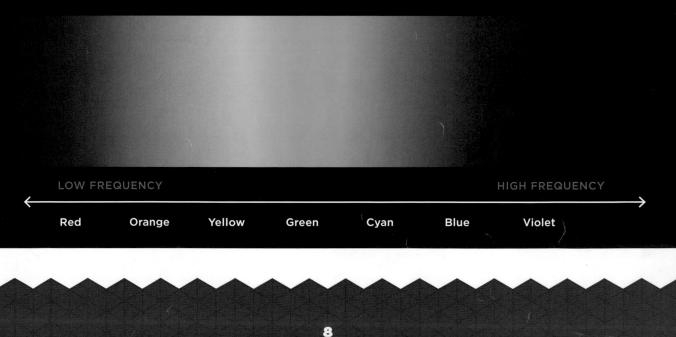

LOW FREQUENCY → HIGH FREQUENCY

Red   Orange   Yellow   Green   Cyan   Blue   Violet

FROM LINE TO LOOP

The ends of a color line can be joined together to form a loop. The brain adds the color magenta where the ends meet. Magenta is made of both red and violet frequencies. It is between red and violet on the loop. This loop of colors is called the color wheel.

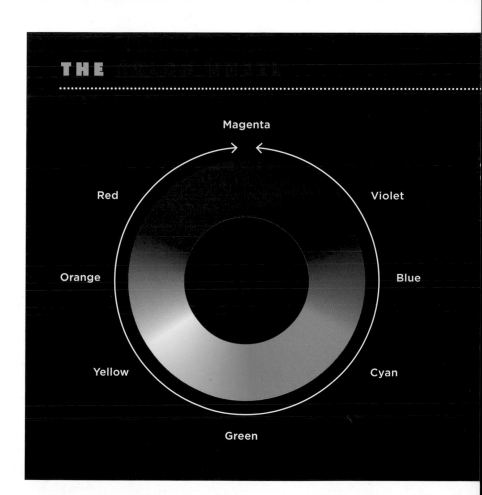

THE COLOR WHEEL

Magenta

Red

Violet

Orange

Blue

Yellow

Cyan

Green

PROJECT

1

MAGIC COLOR SPINNER

STUFF YOU'LL NEED

- WHITE POSTER BOARD
- SCISSORS
- RULER
- COMPASS
- GLUE
- PENNY
- BLACK MARKER

TERMS

- COLOR
- FREQUENCY
- CIRCLE

B lack is the absence of color. White is all frequencies of color. What happens when you flash black and white before your eyes? You get a lot of crazy colors! Try this project to see it happen.

HOW TO MAKE IT

1 Use the compass to draw two circles on the poster board. Keep the compass at the same setting for both circles.

2 Cut the circles out. Glue them together. Let the glue dry.

3 Use the ruler to draw a line through the center of the circle.

4 Color half of the circle with the black marker. Use the ruler to keep the halves separate.

5 Draw some curved lines on the white half of the circle.

6   Use scissors to make a cut in the center of the circle. The cut should be a little less than ¾ inch (1.9 cm) long.

7   **Insert** the penny halfway into the cut.

8   Hold the circle by the penny. Place it on a flat surface and spin it like a top.

9   Watch for new colors as the top spins. Everyone watching will see different colors. That's because the colors are created in your brain!

OPPOSITE COLORS
TAKE IT AS A COMPLEMENT!

Every color has a complementary color. Complementary colors are on opposite sides of the color wheel. Pick a color on the wheel. Look straight across the wheel. That color is the complement of the color you picked.

Stare at a color on the wheel for 60 seconds. Then look at a plain white wall. The complementary color will appear! This is called an afterimage. Afterimages happen when your eyes tire of seeing one color.

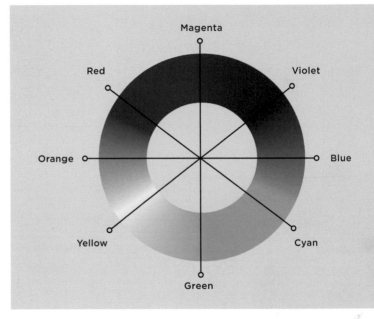

There are different kinds of color wheels. They are all very similar. But some include colors used for specific purposes such as painting or printing.

Stare at the pink square on the right for 60 seconds. Then look at a white surface. A green afterimage should appear.

Afterimages work with photos too! Stare at the image on the left for 60 seconds. Then look at a white surface. What do you see?

16

PROJECT

2 AFTERIMAGE ILLUSIONS

◆◆◆◆◆◆◆

Create your own afterimage **illusion**! In this project, you'll learn to make afterimages in two different ways. The colors won't look right until you see the afterimage!

STUFF YOU'LL NEED

- 1 SHEET ORANGE PAPER
- 2 SHEETS WHITE PAPER
- 1 SHEET MAGENTA PAPER
- BLACK MARKER
- GLUE STICK
- SCISSORS
- COMPUTER
- IMAGE EDITING PROGRAM

TERMS

- AFTERIMAGE
- COLOR
- TRIANGLE
- CIRCLE
- COMPLEMENTARY COLOR

PAPER AFTERIMAGE

1. Cut two or three triangles out of a sheet of white paper.

2. Glue the triangles to the orange paper.

3. Color in the tops of the triangles with black marker. They should look like mountaintops.

4. Cut a circle out of the magenta paper. Glue it to the orange paper above the mountains.

5. Place the second sheet of white paper next to your picture. Stare at the middle of your picture for 60 seconds. Then look at the white paper. What do you see?

COMPUTER AFTERIMAGE

You can make great **afterimages** with a computer and an image editing program. Adobe Photoshop is an example of an image editing program.

1 Open any photo in the image editing program.

2 Locate the **"invert"** function. In Photoshop, it's in the "image" **menu** under "adjustments."

3 Invert the image. This will change all the colors to their complements.

4 Print the inverted image. Tape it to a white wall. Stare at the image for 60 seconds. Then look at the white wall. What do you see?

3-D OR NOT 3-D?
THE OBJECTS THAT COULDN'T BE

The drawings on these pages look 3-D. But look at them more closely. They couldn't really exist as objects. It takes a moment to realize that the shapes are actually **illusions**. These impossible shapes can only exist on paper.

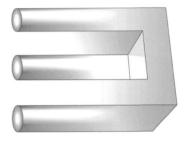

A BLIVET

IMPOSSIBLE OBJECTS

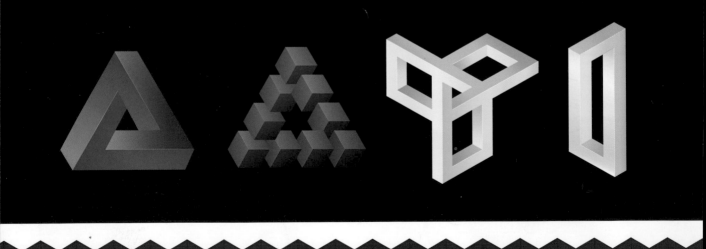

A blivet is one example of an impossible shape. It looks like a fork. You can see the start of two **prongs** on the right side. But on the left side, there are three prongs. How did that happen? Look closely. The middle prong is not attached to the outside prongs. So this shape couldn't exist.

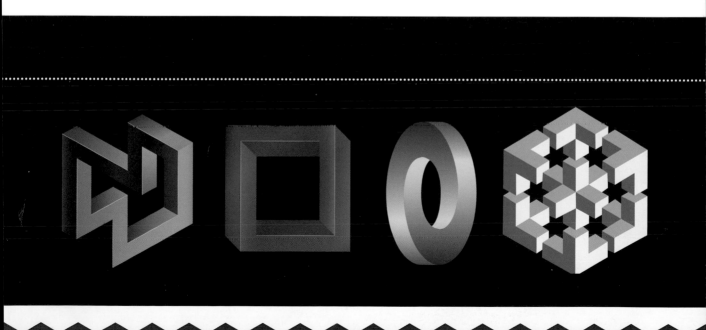

PROJECT

3

DRAWING IMPOSSIBLE OBJECTS

STUFF YOU'LL NEED

- PENCIL
- ERASER
- PAPER

TERMS

- 3-D
- 2-D
- TRIANGLE
- PARALLEL
- OVAL
- HORIZONTAL
- VERTICAL

Impossible objects are **paradox illusions**. The brain wants to make them 3-D, but they can only exist in 2-D. Try drawing two of the coolest impossible objects. The Penrose triangle and the blivet are easy and fun to draw. Then make up your own impossible objects.

THE PENROSE TRIANGLE

1 Draw a triangle on a sheet of paper.

2 Draw a second triangle around the first triangle.

3 Go back to the inner triangle. Extend one end of each side halfway to the outer triangle.

4 Starting at the end of each extended side, draw lines parallel to the sides of the triangles. The parallel lines should go all the way to the outer triangle.

5 Erase the tips of the outer corners. Replace each with a single line that closes the shape.

THE BLIVET

1 Draw three ovals at the top of a sheet of paper. Make the ovals short and wide. Space them the same distance apart.

2 Draw a vertical line down from the left side of each oval. Make the lines the same length.

▶ 3 Draw vertical lines down from the right sides of the ovals. Make the lines from the outer ovals longer than the lines from step 2. Make the line from the middle oval shorter than the lines from step 2.

▶ 4 Connect the two longest vertical lines with a horizontal line. Then connect the right two medium-length lines with a horizontal line.

5 Draw a horizontal line from the end of the shortest vertical line to the line to its left.

▶ 6 Connect the end of the leftmost line to the end of the line to its right. Connect the end of the shortest vertical line to the end of the line to its right.

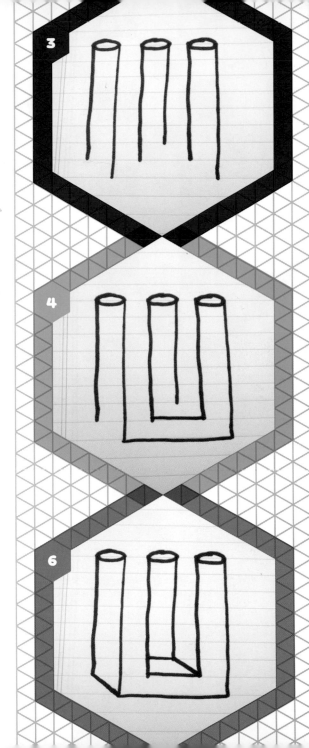

25

PROJECT 4

DISTORTING ILLUSIONS

◆ ◆ ◆ ◆ ◆ ◆ ◆ ◆

STUFF YOU'LL NEED

- GRAPH PAPER
- BLACK MARKER
- WHITE PAINT PEN
- SCISSORS
- COLORED PAPER
- GLUE

TERMS

- PATTERN
- HORIZONTAL
- SQUARE
- VERTICAL

Distorting illusions are a type of **cognitive** illusion. Learn two ways to make straight lines look curved.

The wavy checkerboard has dots in the squares. The dots make the paper look like it's bending. The cafe wall illusion has a staggered checkerboard pattern. The red horizontal lines seem to bend up and down!

WAVY CHECKERBOARD

1 Fill in four squares of graph paper with a black marker. The four squares should form a larger square.

2 Continue filling in large black squares in a checkerboard pattern. Fill one whole sheet.

3 Add two white dots to each black square. Put the dots in opposite corners. On some squares put them in the bottom-left and upper-right corners. On others, put dots in the bottom-right and upper-left squares. Group similar dot patterns together.

4 Hold the finished checkerboard at arm's length. The straight pattern will look wavy!

CAFE WALL ILLUSION

1 Use a black marker to make thick vertical stripes on graph paper. Make them all the same width and the same distance apart.

2 Cut the paper horizontally into strips. Cut along the lines of the graph paper. The strips can be different widths.

3 Glue the strips to a sheet of colored paper. Leave a little space between them. Every other strip should be one small graph square to the right.

4 When finished, the straight lines look bent!

POLK SCHOOL
LIBRARY MEDIA CENTER

2-D - flat or having only two dimensions, such as length and width.

3-D - having length, width, and height and taking up space.

AFTERIMAGE - a visual sensation that appears after looking at one image for an extended time.

CIRCLE - a curved line in which every point on the line is the same distance from the center.

COLOR - a frequency of light seen as a certain hue.

COMPLEMENT - the color opposite from another color on a color wheel.

FREQUENCY - the number of sound or light waves that pass one point within a certain time.

HORIZONTAL - in the same direction as the ground, or side-to-side.

LIGHT - radiation that is visible to the human eye.

OVAL - a two-dimensional egg shape.

PARALLEL - lying or moving in the same direction but always the same distance apart.

PATTERN - one or more things that repeat in a recognizable way.

SQUARE - a shape with four straight, equal sides and four equal angles.

TRIANGLE - a shape with three straight sides.

VERTICAL - in the opposite direction from the ground, or up-and-down.

GLOSSARY

COGNITIVE - having to do with mental activities such as thinking, remembering, and imagining.

DISTORT - to twist out of a natural or normal shape.

ILLUSION - something that appears real, but is not.

INSERT - to stick something into something else.

INVERT - to reverse the order or relationship of something.

MENU - a list of things to choose from.

OVERSTIMULATED - having received too much of something, such as light or sound, that affects the senses or other bodily functions.

PARADOX - something that seems to be both possible and impossible.

PHYSIOLOGICAL - having to do with the way the body works.

PRONG - one of the sharp points of a fork, tool, or antler.

SLANT - to lean or be at an angle, especially to slope up or down.

WEB SITES

To learn more about math and science, visit ABDO Publishing Company on the World Wide Web at www.abdopublishing.com. Web sites about creative ways for kids to experience math and science are featured on our Book Links page. These links are routinely monitored and updated to provide the most current information available.

INDEX